Twilight of Divine Right

From Defenestration to Restoration: Wargame Rules for 1618 to 1660

Nicholas Dorrell

The Pike & Shot Society

*Twilight of
Divine Right*

The Pike & Shot Society

14 Barton Road
Hornchurch
Essex
RM12 4AA
United Kingdom

Website: www.pikeandshot.org

The *Pike and Shot Society* was founded in 1973 with the aim of promoting interest in, and the study of, warfare during the Early Modern period. As well as producing specialist studies such as this book, it publishes its own journal, *Arquebusier*, six times a year. For more information on the Society, please contact the above address or see our website.

Paperback
ISBN: 978-1-902768-50-2

Front & Rear Cover: Design by Nicholas Dorrell & Iain Stanford
Design & Layout dennis@kavitagraphics.co.uk

Twilight of Divine Right: Table of Contents

Twilight of
Divine Right

Acknowledgements

The ancestor of these rules was written by Steven Thomas in 1995, then revised and re-published by Andrew Coleby in 2005. The first Pike and Shot Society version appeared in 2008 as *Twilight of the Sun King*. I would like to take the opportunity to thank both Steven and Andrew for their kind permission to continue their efforts into this work.

I would also like to thank two fellow Pike & Shot Society members for their contributions. Once again, thanks to Iain Stanford for his invaluable assistance with the maps and generally in the production of this booklet. Without his assistance this work would literally not have been possible. I would also like to thank Tim Allen and John Burn for rewriting parts of the text and for their help in shaping and structuring it.

Finally, I would like to thank the members of Wyre Forest Wargames Club for testing the numerous rules changes, half-baked ideas and scenarios I came up with.

Despite the best efforts of others, any errors that may remain within the work are solely the responsibility of the author.

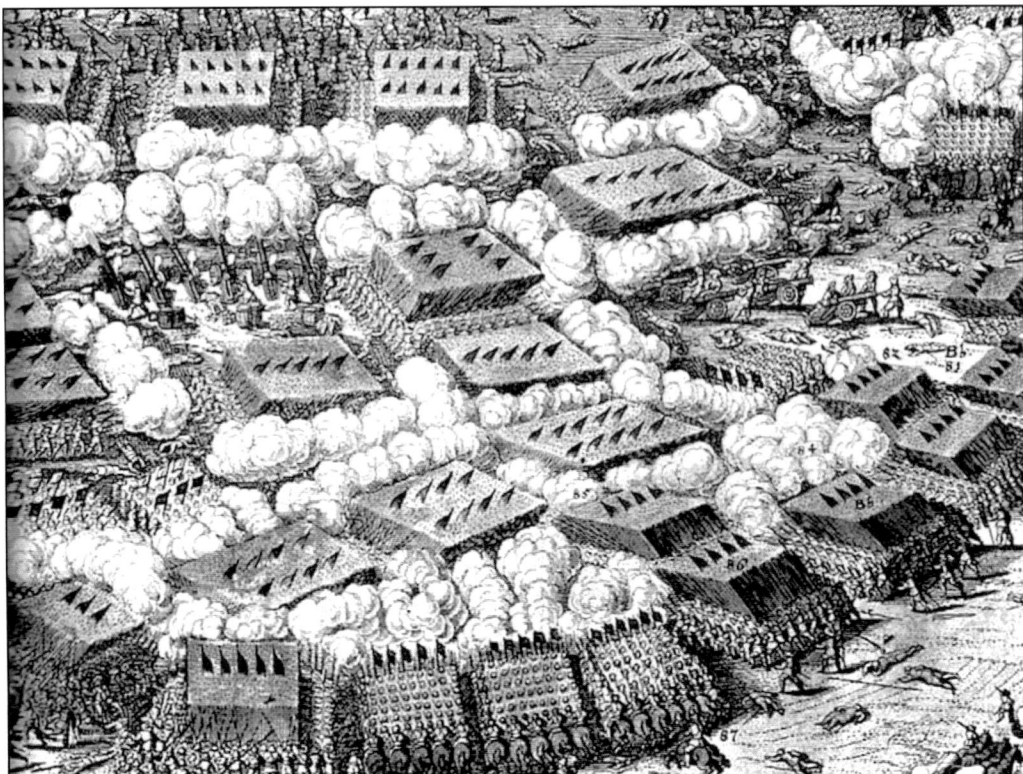

Stylised Picture of Combat

Design Philosophy

Twilight of Divine Right is adapted from *Twilight of
the Sun King*, a set of wargames rules designed to
provide a simple and enjoyable way for players to
reproduce large horse and musket battles. Whilst
Twilight of the Sun King concerned itself with the age
of Marlborough, this present set shifts the focus to
the first half of the seventeenth century. *Twilight of
Divine Right* concentrates on the Thirty Years' War
and English Civil Wars, though these rules could
cover warfare in Eastern Europe too.

The rules are radical, some would say
reductionist, in their conception. The premise is that
morale rather than casualties was the key to deciding
the outcome of battles. Many wargames rules pay
lip-service to this idea but these rules take the
radical step of collapsing shooting and close combat
into morale. This dramatically simplifies game play
but does so, in the designers' opinion, without
significant loss of historical accuracy.

In the area of command and control, these rules
are based on the idea that the armies of this era were
'arthritic' in their manoeuvring, but seldom actually
paralysed. In game terms, this means that, while it is
possible for units to move forward, more complex
actions may not be feasible, especially if morale has
become degraded. There is no facility for recovering
morale under these rules. The crucial skill for the

players, like the generals of the time, is to not push
frontline units too far and progressively replace
worn-down units with fresh ones at the crucial stage
or area of the battle.

Most historic battles can be played with 1 or 2
players a side on a reasonably sized table and in a
single gaming session.

For further support you can join either one of the
following Yahoo Groups:

The Pike and Shot Society
(You need to be a member to join):
https://groups.yahoo.com/neo/groups/
PikeandShotSociety/info

and the Twilight of the Sun King
https://groups.yahoo.com/neo/groups/
TwilightSK/info

and/or the Wyre Forest Wargamers forum
http://wfgamers.freeforums.net

It would be useful for people interested in the
rules to join these groups since it will provide you
with direct access to the authors and additional
support material that may be produced in the future
via the files section.

Nicholas Dorrell, 2018

Twilight of Divine Right

Equipment

Opposing armies

Any scale of wargames figures can be used. The author favours 6mm figures himself, but that is personal preference. Figures need to be mounted on bases of the same size, but it doesn't matter what the size is. Another approach is to make counters out of card; this is quick and cheap, and allows players to experiment with the rules before committing themselves.

Terrain

Model scenery—trees, hills, and so on is ideal. Again, if you are using card counters, you could draw the battlefield map or copy it from one of the accompanying scenario books.

Dice

Two ordinary dice (hereafter known as D6, numbered 1 2 3 4 5 6).

For Morale tests, some players might wish to use two average dice instead (numbered 2 3 3 4 4 5). If you do not have any average dice, you could roll a D6 but a roll of a 1 counts as a 3 and a roll of a 6 counts as a 4.

Bombardment Markers

We use a puff of smoke (cotton wool) but anything similar would be fine.

Morale Markers

These could be distinctive dice placed by a unit and turned to show the appropriate value or they could be multiple markers or counters.

Measuring

Tape measures are fine. Some players prefer wooden rods (dowelling) or card that is marked off in game measures (see Base Widths, below).

Pike Drill

Scales and Sizes

Ground Scale

All Troop bases in *Twilight of Divine Right* must be the same width. These base widths govern the way in which all distances are measured. Within these rules we will refer to **Base Widths** asBWs.

BWs will be referred to in both the movement and the firing rules in either fractions or multiples as follows:

- ½BW = ½ Base width in distance
- 1BW = 1 Base width in distance
- 2BW = 2 Base widths in distance, and so on.

It is up to players to determine the standard base widths of their armies. We recommend a standard base width of **60mm** since this base width will enable most historical battles to be fought on tables 1.8 metres by 1.2 metres (6 foot by 4 foot) to 2.4 metres by 1.8 metres (8 foot by 6 foot).

Unit Scale

1BW is approximately 150 metres.

A unit represents a regiment or its equivalent which equates to approximately 1,000 to 2,000 infantry or 500 to 800 cavalry. Although it is treated as a single unit for gaming purposes, in reality, an infantry regiment would be deployed in two (perhaps more) battalia and cavalry would be in several squadrons.

- 1 artillery unit is used for each 4–8 guns or part thereof in the army.
- 1 siege artillery unit is used for each 5 guns or part thereof in the army.

Unit Sizes

Historical units could and did vary in size. Types of unit varied in numbers too. An infantry unit that is a 'Regiment' represents about 1,000 men, while an infantry unit that is 'Tercio' represents 1,500 men. Further variation is introduced in two additional unit size ratings, 'Large' and 'Small'.

'Large' Units

A 'Large' unit is approximately 20% bigger than the standard unit so a regiment represents approximately 1,200 infantry.

A Large unit receives one additional allowable morale failure (see **Morale Fails and Routs** below): it gets 4 morale fails, instead of the usual 3.

'Small' Units

A 'Small' unit is approximately 20% smaller than the standard unit so a 'Small' 'Regiment' unit represents approximately 800 infantry.

A Small unit receives a minus dice modifier when taking morale tests.

Approximate Unit Sizes

Type	Standard	Small	Large
Early Tercio	2,000	1,600	2,400
Tercio/ Swedish Brigade	1,500	1,200	1,800
Regiment	1,000	800	1,200
Harquebusier	800	640	960
Cuirassier	600	480	720
All other mounted	500	400	600
Artillery (guns)	4 to 8	3 to 6	5 to 10

Unit Basing

Infantry and cavalry units each have two bases of figures.

Artillery units are represented by a single base.

It is possible to play with any basing arrangement in a unit so long as theBW measurement is half the frontage of an infantry or cavalry unit.

The number of figures or models on a base makes no difference to the game and the player can use as many or few as desired.

Base proportions
- Early Tercio, Light Horse, Artillery: **1BW by 1BW**
- Other Infantry & Cavalry: **1BW wide by ½BW deep**
- Command: **½BW by ½BW**

The depth of **bases** may be deeper to accommodate the models used.

Players may choose to represent deployed and limbered artillery with separate bases but usually only a deployed gun model and crew will be required. It is suggested that players do not glue gun models to bases, so that abandoned artillery units can be represented.

We would recommend that players vary the number of figures on command bases to represent both the rank and quality of the commander. Players may also use any scale or measure as long as all troop bases are consistent.

Troop Types

Twilight of
Divine Right

Units are of a few main types but there is differentiation within that. Infantry units, for instance, are defined further by the ratio of muskets and pikes within the unit; cavalry may have attached groups of shot.

Infantry Units

All unit types that fight on foot are referred to as Infantry Units. Infantry are armed with a combination of pike or shot weapons.

Pike to Firearm Ratio

Type	Standard
M	All or nearly all of the unit are armed with muskets
MH	The unit has around 2 muskets to 1 pike.
MX	The unit has around 3 muskets to 2 pikes.
PH	The unit has around 1 musket to 1 pike
'a'	Unit's firearms mostly arquebus *(reduces fire superiority rank)*

Arquebusiers (a)

These units have mostly or all arquebuses, rather than muskets. A lower case 'a' before the above rating denotes them e.g. a unit with 3 firearms, mainly arquebuses, to 2 pike would be noted as 'aMX'.

Having arquebuses reduces the unit's fire superiority rank.

Infantry Formations

There are four main types of infantry formations – Early Tercio, Tercio, Regiment and Swedish Brigade. These are classifications for the purposes of the game and may or may not relate to historic names e.g. an historical unit called a tercio could be an 'Early Tercio' in the early period of the Thirty Years' War, a 'Tercio' in the middle period, then at the end of war it could be a 'Regiment'.

Early Tercio (ET)

A mixed unit of mainly pikes and firearms deployed 12 or more ranks deep. Mainly used by Tilly's army up until his death in early 1632.

ET units always count as having rear support and are less worried about threats to their flank or rear. They are difficult to manoeuvre and fail some Action Tests on a roll of 1 to 4.

ET units rout on their 5th morale fail.

Tercio (Tc)

A mixed unit of mainly pikes and firearms deployed 8 to 10 ranks deep, which became the standard formation of many armies, especially Catholic armies in the Thirty Years' War up to 1630, but increasingly replaced after that time.

Tc units are less worried than most other units about threats to their flank or rear. They are difficult to manoeuvre and fail some Action Tests on a roll of 1 to 3.

Tc units rout on their 4th morale fail.

Regiment (Rt)

A 6 ranks deep infantry formation usually of mainly pikes and firearms but sometimes of only firearms. Used at first mainly by Protestant armies in the Thirty Years' War but widely used by all armies after 1634 and this became the standard formation of all armies and was the standard English Civil War formation.

Rt units rout on their 3rd morale fail.

Swedish Brigade (SB)

This was a complicated formation of interlocking groups of pikemen and musketeers. It was used by the Swedes from 1630 to 1634. It demanded a high level of training and was abandoned after the battle of Nördlingen, 1634.

They use Defensive Fire when units attempt to contact them.

SB units rout on their 4th morale fail.

Special Rule: A SB unit's weapon ratio is not set and can be changed during the game, the flexible formation allows different combinations to be emphasised. They can choose to be rated as MH, MX or PH. At the start of the game the owning player states what rating they are. During any subsequent movement phase of the player they may attempt to change a unit's rating. Roll a D6 and on 3+ they can change (this is not an Action Test). Only one attempt per turn can be made to change the unit's rating.

Swedish Brigade Example: The player has taken a defensive stance at the start of a game with some Swedish Brigade units and declares that they are set up as MH units. They have regimental guns and so will fire a firepower rank 1, see below, and have a good chance of receiving the +1 morale test bonus for a better firepower rank in a fire fight. The opposing player moves some MX units into firing range to attack the Swedish Brigades. The opposing player soon

realises his mistake as the better firepower of the Swedish Brigades means he gets the worst of the situation. Therefore, he attempts to close into contact where the Swedish Brigades firepower won't count and they will receive a -1 on morale tests because they are inferior in melee power, see below. But the Swedish Brigades have defensive fire and so the attacking units will need 4 or better to move into contact, they roll and fail. The player with the Swedish Brigade now sees that he is potentially vulnerable and so decides to change his units from MH to MX. As MX units they will still receive the firepower bonus but will no longer receive the -1 in contact. They roll to do this and succeed.

After a few more turns the enemy is weakened and the player with the Swedish Brigades decides it is time to attack. He therefore decides to change his stance again, this time to PH. This will give him an advantage in contact so he plans to then move into contact. He can do both because changing stance does not count as Action Test or movement, but failure to change stance might mean second thoughts. So the first unit successfully changes stance and then takes an Action Test to move into contact. The second unit tries to change stance but fails. It can still try to close but will do so as an MX unit.

Special Characteristics:

Assault Tactics (AT)

Representing the tactic of firing a salvo and then immediately charging into combat. Used from 1635 by Weimarian, French and Swedish units. Also used by some English Civil War units at some battles – Montrose's Irish units, the Royalists at Naseby for example.

Being AT gives an opposing unit a -1 modifier if the AT unit moved into contact from with firing range.

Axe armed (a)

Pikeless infantry who have a large axe to defend themselves with e.g. Russian Streltzi, Polish infantry, are noted as 'Ma'. If armed with arquebuses it would be an 'aMa' unit.

'Ma' units do not receive the extra -1 in melee in the open that M units do.

Regimental Guns (RG)

A small number (1 to 4) of very light guns attached to an infantry formation to provide close support. These were popularised by the Swedes when they intervened in the Thirty Years War and then copied by others. After 1635 their popularity declined and they became less common over time.

A unit with RG receives a bonus e.g. an MX unit with firepower of 3 counts as 2 if it has RGs. RGs can be lost. If a unit with RG moves more than ½BW, then it takes an Action Test (+1 dice modifier if the move was 1BW or less); if it fails, then the unit loses its RG.

Unit Rating Example: A Trained, MX, Small, RG, Tercio is a unit 8 to 10 ranks deep with about 3 muskets to pike. It is understrength but has attached light artillery pieces.

Cavalry Units

There are six main types of cavalry (note that dragoons are not classed as cavalry, even though they have horses).

Gallopers (Ga)

Charge at the gallop, but generally in poor order, and prone to uncontrolled pursuit e.g. Finnish 'Hackapells', Royalists in 1642, units armed with lances.

Ga units give an extra minus to units that they charge but receive pluses on their chance to pursue and distance they will pursue. They cannot fire unless fired upon.

Ga units rout on their 2nd morale fail.

Swedish School (Sw)

Charge at the trot, firing a pistol as they close. This tactic was used by Swedish cavalry and was copied by many others. Oxford Royalist cavalry used it from 1643 and most English cavalry by the end of the Civil War.

Sw cavalry give a minus to others when they charge into contact. They cannot fire unless fired upon.

Sw units rout on their 2nd morale fail.

Dutch School (Du)

Attempt to disrupt their target by firing pistols, then charge at the trot if successful. Commonly used by Protestants in the Thirty Years War. Many Parliamentarian cavalry used this until later in the war.

Du cavalry use Defensive Fire when charged. They normally get no bonus when charging but do if they charge a mounted unit that fails to charge them. They can fire.

Du units rout on their 2nd morale fail.

Cuirassiers (Cu)

Clad in three-quarter armour and often fought in relatively deep formations. They fired their pistols to disrupt their target and would charge after firing. Commonly used in the Thirty Years War, particularly by Catholic armies, but less so after 1635. They were expensive to maintain and not very manoeuvrable. Later cuirassier units are often better classified as Dutch or Swedish school cavalry as they changed to a similar style to these types.

Cu cavalry give a minus to others when they charge into contact. Because of their size and armour they have an extra morale failure. This is also why they are difficult to manoeuvre and fail some Action Tests on a roll of 1 to 3.

Cu units rout on their 3rd morale fail.

Harquebusiers (Hq)

Cavalry who fired mounted in support of other units. Popular at the start of the Thirty Years War, but disappeared as a type as they were converted to dragoons or conventional cavalry. Later Harquebusiers can be classified as Poor (see below), as Cuirassiers or as Dutch or Swedish school. Any cavalry that is reluctant to charge and instead relies on firing could be classified as H.

They can fire and get the Defensive Fire bonus when charged but never get a bonus for charging. Since their role is to fire, they are not as affected by incoming fire as other cavalry so do not receive a minus when fired upon. Because of their size Hq units have an extra morale failure. This is also why they are difficult to manoeuvre and fail some Action Tests on a roll of 1 to 3.

Hq units rout on their 3rd morale fail.

Light Horse (LH)

Skirmishing cavalry, such as Croats, 'Poles', Hungarians. On the battlefield they are useful in supporting roles but they are vulnerable if contacted.

They can fire but receive minuses for being in melee. They can withdraw if contacted and also perform many manoeuvres without an Action Test.

LH rout on their 2nd morale fail.

Commanded Shot (CS)

Groups of musketeers (usually 50 to 200 men) attached to cavalry to give fire support. This idea was popularised by the Swedes and copied by others.

A unit with CS can fire and gives a unit that can already fire a bonus. The unit can use Defensive Fire. If unit with CS moves more than 1.5BW they take an Action Test, if a fail they are lost. The CS are lost if unit falls back from melee.

Poor cavalry (P)

These are units that are either using ineffective tactics or suffering some other combat disadvantage e.g. poorly mounted cavalry. Poor cavalry are not necessarily low-quality units, although some may be, they are just relatively ineffective in combat when compared to other cavalry. It is possible for a unit to be Elite and Poor cavalry, i.e. a high morale unit using bad tactics. One example would be Scottish and Irish cavalry in the British Civil Wars. These will usually be classified as PC. Another example is later Harquebusiers who are now using tactics similar to Cuirassiers. This could count as Poor Cuirassiers.

Other Units

Dragoons (Dr)

In this period, dragoons (Dr) generally moved on horseback but fought on foot. They could fight mounted, but at a disadvantage.

They can fire. They suffer a minus if contacted mounted but can dismount without penalty.

Dr units rout on their 2nd morale fail.

Artillery

Artillery Units during this period were normally heavy and their organisation was primitive. These units are therefore difficult to move and usually static once positioned. These units must start any game deployed unless specifically noted in a scenario. Artillery Units are divided into two types, which are as follows:

Field Artillery (FG):

Usually guns between 3 to 12pdr. Also larger, siege, guns which count as FG but less of them make a unit.

Light Artillery (LG):

Small guns, usually under 3pdr; sometimes having multiple small barrels; leather guns and similar lightweight pieces used as a battery, rather than attached to units.

FG and LG units rout on their 1st morale fail if in contact with an opposing unit, otherwise on their 2nd morale fail.

Baggage

Usually, baggage is placed behind an army, on its baseline. Its purpose is to show the direction for pursuit. A model wagon on a 1BW by 1BW base is recommended and looks the part, but is not essential so long as both sides agree to mark the location in some other way.

Generals

An army always has one general who is the Army Commander. According to its size, it may have a number of Wing Commanders too; they command "Wings" which are permanent subdivisions of the army.

Generals and Army Size

Units	Up to 10	11-15	16-20	21 or more
Army Commanders	1	1	1	1
Wing Commanders	0	1	2	3

Function

Generals are used to give bonus moves, extra attempts to pass Action Tests, and to influence the outcome of Army or Wing or Morale tests. The number of these is equivalent to a General's command rating. A general may attempt to override a failed morale check once per turn. The Army Commander can affect any unit; Wing Commanders only affect units under their command.

Ratings of Generals

Rating	0	1	2	3
Definition	Poor	Average	Good	Exceptional

Unit Formations

Infantry and mounted units generally have two formations, Line and March Column. In Line, the two bases are placed adjacent to each other, flanks touching. A March Column looks similar to a line but the unit is facing and moving in the direction of the shortest edge. Use a direction marker or something similar to indicate a unit is in column or turn one of the bases so that the unit looks like a T. If multiple units are in a large March Column then only the first unit needs to be in a T.

Infantry units can form square or hedgehog formation but these were relatively rarely used in this period. It was used when infantry had lost all its cavalry support and was being threatened by enemy cavalry. Most commonly this was when the army had been defeated and isolated infantry were attempting to withdraw from the battlefield. If a single unit forms square or hedgehog, the two bases are placed back to back. Alternatively, a suitable marker can be placed by the unit. For morale test purposes, units in square always have 'secure' flanks and have no flank or rear. They cannot fire or move into combat.

Dragoons can dismount and fight as infantry but they still count as cavalry for the number of morale failures they can suffer. They also will become one size smaller than they would be if mounted. A normal unit that dismounts will become 'Small'. The unit's quality will also usually become one level worse when it dismounts. So, for example, a Trained unit will become Raw; a Raw unit will become Wavering. Dragoons are not downgraded when they dismount, they are units that dismounted to fight. Dragoons can fire ½BW, all other mounted only ¼BW.

Unit Quality

This represents the general level of training and ability of units. There are three levels of quality:

- Raw: Militia, newly raised units and other badly performing troops.
- Trained: Average quality, the vast majority of any army.
- Elite: High quality units.

Determined or Wavering

These additional classifications are used in conjunction with the three basic quality ratings. They are used to designate units who for whatever reason have shown either a greater or lesser commitment to fight but do not warrant an increase or reduction in Unit Quality e.g. a unit can be designated as Elite and Determined or Elite and Wavering.

Musket Drill

- Determined: +1 morale failure (see Morale Fails and Routs below) e.g. a Determined Ga, Du or Sw unit would get 3 morale fails.
- Wavering: -1 morale failure (see Morale Fails and Routs below) e.g. a Wavering foot regiment (Rt) would get 2 morale fails.

Setting Up a Game

These rules include two introductory scenarios. These are the ideal starting point to get to know the rules.

There are also scenario books, covering battles of the Thirty Years War and English Civil War, that accompany these rules. The battles included in each book vary in type and size and, in the case of the Thirty Years War, in opposing forces. A third option is for players to agree to refight an historical battle. A battlefield map will determine terrain and the units can usually be matched from the same source.

Finally, these rules include a dice system for generating English Civil War armies. If this is used, players will need to decide in which year the battle is taking place. Terrain can be placed by agreement or an historical battlefield could be used whilst the actual armies are dice-generated.

In all cases, the two armies must be within bombardment range of each other at the start of the game: at least some of the opposing armies must be within 10BW of each other. Only in encounter games or under special circumstances will this not be the case.

Player Turn Sequence

	Player	Phase	Notes
1.a	A	Generals	Active player moves his generals
1.b	A	Units	Active player moves units, individually or in groups.
			Check if Action test required.
2.	A	Artillery	Active player assigns Bombardment or Firing Targets
3.a	P/A	Unit Morale	Passive units take a morale test as a result of Active player's actions.
			Active player units test for pursuit.
3.b	P	Wing Morale	Passive player: any Wing with half or fewer units remaining must test its morale.
3.c	P	Army Morale	Passive player: if the Army has half or fewer units remaining, it tests its morale.

The game is played in alternate player turns. On his turn, each player is the Active player and his opponent is Passive. At the end of the player turn, these roles are reversed so the Active player is now Passive and vice versa.

First game turn

The game begins with a special first turn. The defender is Active but he begins with phase 2 (he misses out phase 1; there is no movement of units or generals). This represents the initial bombardment as the battle begins.

Movement

➤ A unit may make one normal move each turn that its army is Active.

➤ A moving unit may move any distance up to its maximum allowance.

➤ Movement distances differ according to whether the going is good or bad.

➤ A unit that contacts an enemy unit stops moving.

➤ The nearby presence of an enemy unit has an effect.

➤ Moves may be made either individually or as part of a group.

➤ Moves that are not normal require the passing of an Action Test.

➤ Units or groups may move more than once in a turn by passing an Action Test.

Movement Rates

Type	Formation	Good Going	Bad Going
Infantry	Line	1½BW	½BW
	Column	3BW	1½BW
Cavalry	Line	3BW	None
	Column, Break off, Light Horse	6BW	1½BW
Artillery	Only move if Limbered	1BW	½BW
General		6BW	1½BW

Normal Movement

A normal move by a unit is straight ahead or along a road if in column or limbered artillery. Generals can move freely in any direction desired.

Terrain

Bad going, such as woods, marshes, buildings, steep slopes, slows down movement. The nature of any terrain should be defined in the scenario or agreed by the players before the game starts. They will need to agree which linear obstacles (streams, ditches, etc.) will require an Action Test to cross.

Cavalry has to either dismount or form Column to cross bad going.

Players may agree to vary the Action Test in difficulty to reflect the nature of the terrain.

Moving into Contact with an Enemy

➤ Artillery may not move into contact with an enemy.

➤ Only units in line can move into contact.

➤ The movement to contact must be in a straight line (not wheeling, etc.).

➤ To move into contact with the front edge of an enemy base, an Action Test must be passed (but not to move into contact with the flank or rear edge of an opposing base, except Light Horse).

➤ To count as attacking a flank or rear, the base must start its movement with more than half of its frontage behind a line along the edge of the base.

Charging: Artillery and Units in Column cannot charge. Foot cannot charge cavalry. Rear support units can conform to the movement of a front unit charged.

When a unit moves into contact with an opposing unit, it halts.

Units are then moved so that the edges of the bases align (see diagram below).

- If the target of the charge is mounted then the target is moved so that it is aligned to the charging unit.

- If the target of the charge is on foot then the charging unit is moved so that it is aligned to the target.

- Units providing support or other morale factors to either unit in contact may also be moved (player's choice) to conform with the final alignment of the contacted units.

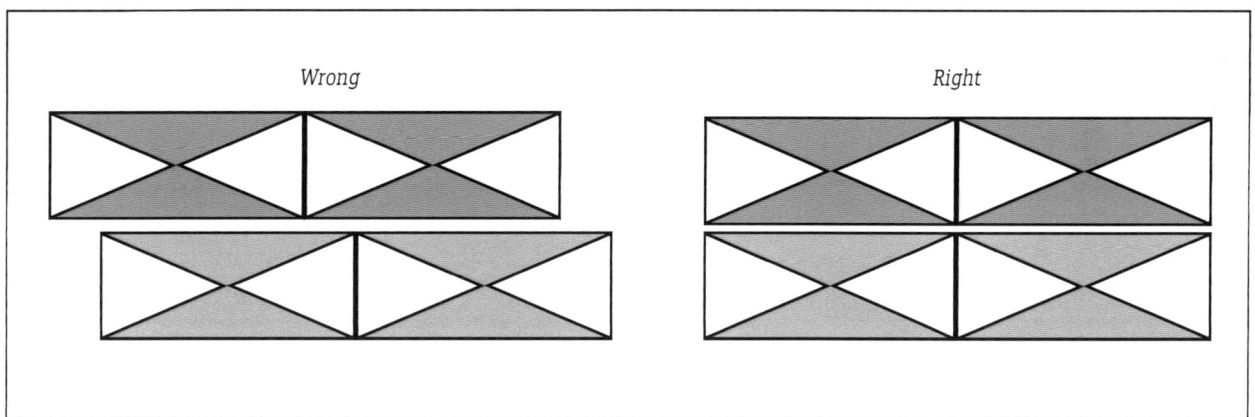

Wrong   *Right*

A unit charged in the flank applies the appropriate morale deductions (see page 19), it aligns the flank or side edge it does not turn to face its opponent. Any movement resulting from unit alignment can be in addition to the normal movement allowance.

Passage of Lines
Any unit can freely pass through or be passed through by generals and artillery.

Units in line can pass through each other without penalty as long as they are facing the same direction. A unit could wheel to face the same direction and then pass through, but this would require it to pass an **Action Test**.

Units in Line and in Combat may about face and pass through any units in line behind them. This requires an **Action Test**, see below. The unit being passed through cannot move in same turn.

Artillery Traversing
Artillery, except siege artillery, can rotate on the spot up to 45 degrees but if it does it cannot fire in the following enemy phase.

Nearby Enemy Units
Each unit exerts a zone of control (ZOC) that extends ½BW forward of the front edge of each base, from one side to the other. Any unit within an enemy unit's ZOC may only move directly towards that unit or directly backwards until out of this zone.

Group Moves
Instead of moving individually, units can move or manoeuvre together as part of a group. The advantage of moving as a group is that all members take just one Action Test so they stay together, they don't get broken up as a result of individual failures and successes. There are some manoeuvres, however, that must be made individually.

All units within a group must be from the same Wing. Each unit must be within 1BW of at least one other unit in the group. Finally, each unit in the group must be facing in the same direction.

Each member of the group must perform exactly the same action. If a player wishes them to perform anything other than identical actions, then the units are not acting as a group so they must be subdivided into smaller groups or individual units and take Action Tests accordingly.

The owning player must specify the units that are attempting to act as a group before the action is rolled for. If the Action Test is passed, then all units perform the same action.

Action Tests

A unit can make one normal move per turn. To make additional moves, or more complex moves, an Action Test must be passed.

A General may use his skill level rating to enable units to conduct additional actions. Units must be within 3BW of the General and be under his command. One Bonus Move or Movement Action Test is permitted per skill level of the General, so a general rated 2 can enable two additional actions.

- execute a failed Action Test
- an entirely new action
- an extra straight ahead or other move

Units that move more than once cannot inflict a morale test on an opponent, nor give a morale modifier in any tests. If the unit did not move because of a failed Action Test, that does not count as a move for this purpose.

Each bullet pointed move is classed as a separate action and cannot be combined with another action unless they are classed as a condition (see below). The exception to this is that a unit changing formation

may wheel as part of its allowed movement but require an additional Action Test to do so.

Individual or Group moves that do not require an Action Test, unless as a 2nd or subsequent move
- A move straight ahead
- Unit in Line charging into contact against a Flank or Rear (except Light Horse, who must take a test)
- Light Horse moving and including a wheel (up to 45 degrees in Line)
- Light Horse doing an about face (180 degrees)

Individual Unit moves that do require an action Test
- Moving into contact (except against Flank or Rear) (columns cannot charge)
- Light Horse charging against a Flank or Rear
- Pull back for Light Horse charged
- Move straight backwards up to half movement, retaining facing**
- If a unit is giving rear support to a unit but not directly aligned or it is giving rear support to a directly adjacent unit and wants to replace a forward unit*
- If in combat to pass through units behind up to half movement distance*
- Sheltering crew return to guns (-1 per enemy unit within 3BW).

Individual or Group Moves that require an Action Test
- Change Formation and then move up to half the new movement distance. A unit will change from Line to Column of vice versa by turning 90 degrees**
- Face to Flank (Turn 90 degrees) in the same formation**
- Move including a wheel (up to 45 degrees in Line) unless Light Horse*
- About Face (180 degrees) unless Light Horse (see above)
- Limber/Unlimber Artillery
- Mount/Dismount Cavalry
- A Swedish Brigade wants to change its musket/pike ratio
- If unit has RG and moves ½BW or more, +1 dice modifier if 1BW or less

- If a unit with CS moves more than 1 ½BW, fails means CS are lost
- Make a bonus (extra) move straight ahead

* The combination of these two actions can be used to replace a front line unit with a rear support. The unit in the front line must always take an Action Test. *If the supporting unit only has to move straight forward it does not need to take an Action Test.* If it has to move to the side up to the unit's frontage before moving forward to replace the front unit then both must take an Action Test. Test for the front unit first and only test for the other if the front unit succeeds.

** These actions and those marked * count as difficult. T, C and H receive a -1 dice modifier. ET units receive a -2 dice modifier.

A Condition:

A condition is classed as separate to a move since it represents situations that may be detrimental to a unit or group attempting to move. **In addition to any Action Test roll required (or not) for movement the player must take additional Action Tests for each occasion the following listed conditions apply to the unit.** Normally they are taken in sequence as the reason for them happens. If the unit fails a test, then all subsequent tests are abandoned and the unit is moved to the point of failure.

Example: A unit is attempting to Charge, it is in a marsh (bad going), it then crosses a stream and is under bombardment. This requires 4 Action Tests. 1 for the bombardment, 1 for the marsh, 1 for crossing the stream and 1 for the charge. Bombardment Action Tests are always the first taken and the rest then in sequence.

Forming Square or Hedgehog:

Forming a square or hedgehog takes a unit 2 turns. The player declares he is forming a square on the turn he starts to form square it. The square is formed during the following turn, no other movement can take place in the two turns.

Any unit attempting to form square will automatically fail a morale test if they are within ½BW of an enemy unit. If the square is contacted by an enemy unit prior to its completion the process is broken and the unit is placed in Line, where they currently are and facing the enemy.

Unit conditions that require an Action Test
- Attempting any type of move or charge with a unit under bombardment.
- Attempting to move or charge through or across terrain defined as bad going or terrain that requires an Action Test to cross.

A conditional Action Test does not require a General to use his rating.

Action Test

Owning player rolls 1d6, adding or subtracting these modifiers...

-1 failed morale test last turn	-1 if trying to contact frontally a unit with Defensive Fire
-1 if Tc, Cu or Hq unit taking a difficult test	-2 if ET unit taking a difficult test

Testing Unit is...	Fail	Succeed
Foot/Cavalry/Artillery (unless limbering)	2 (or less)	3 (or more)
Artillery if limbering	5 (or less)	6 (or more)

Assigning Artillery Targets

Artillery can perform three kinds of fire: **bombardment**, **flank or fire support** and **direct fire**. Artillery can fire up to 10BW and has a 45 degrees angle of fire. Light Guns can only fire up to 3BW and may never bombard.

All artillery fire ignores the presence of friendly units in the line of fire. The units are not solid bodies of troops and artillery is more spread out than depicted. It is assumed that the artillery is firing through the gaps in the units and/or are taking advantage of minor rises not depicted on the table. Certain terrain will block line of fire – woods, hills, villages/towns for example.

In general, artillery must target frontline enemy units. If the target is on higher ground though, it can be targeted. If the artillery is firing from higher ground it can target any unit on lower ground it can hit.

Bombarding

Bombarding is fire by artillery designed to disrupt movement. Bombarding is performed by a single unit at ranges above 3BW and up to 10BW. Bombarding forces the target to take an Action Test when it wouldn't normally, or an additional Action Test if it needs one anyway.

Example: a unit being bombarded by one opposing gun wishes to move straight ahead. This normally does not need an Action Test but now it does because the unit is being bombarded. If the unit wished to move and wheel, which normally requires an Action Test, it would have to take two: one for being bombarded and another for wheeling.

Direct Fire

Direct Fire causes a Morale test (not an Action Test). Direct Fire is performed by one (or more guns) at ranges up to 3BW but must be performed by at least two guns at ranges of 3BW to 10BW (only one gun would be bombarding). When direct firing the gun

or guns are themselves causing the morale test. The target will also have to take an Action Test when it wouldn't normally, or an additional Action Test if it needs one anyway.

Supporting Fire

To provide flank or fire support the testing unit must be taking a morale test for some other reason (this could be other guns firing at it). The support fire will then give a -1 modifier for each gun targeting the opposing unit. Flank support is defined below and in general terms is when the unit is along side to the flank of the unit taking the test. Fire support is when the gun is in its angle of fire and up to 10BW away. In both cases a single gun provides a -1 modifier per gun.

Artillery Use Example: The player has two field guns, FG's. In the early turns no opposing unit is within 3BW and neither is any other unit causing an Action Test. Therefore the guns can target a unit each and force them to take additional Action Tests. Alternatively if they can both fire at a single opposing unit they can cause that unit to take a morale test. If the player had a 3rd gun that was eligible to hit the same targeted unit then all three guns could hit it and make it take a morale test with a -1 in addition to any other relevant modifiers.

Later in the game one of the FG's has an opposing unit within 3BW that it can target. In addition there are a number of opposing units which will have to take a test because of the actions of other units. Both guns still have the options as earlier in the game of bombarding any unit as above if they wish. More commonly the player will choose to Direct Fire or give Supporting Fire. The FG which has an opposing unit within 3BW may direct fire at it and make it take a morale test and Action Tests is it moves. It does not have to do this and can choose another option if it wishes. Either unit can provide supporting fire, give a -1, to any opposing unit which is taking a morale test because of the actions of other units. The 2nd FG can provide supporting fire to the 1st FG if it is direct firing.

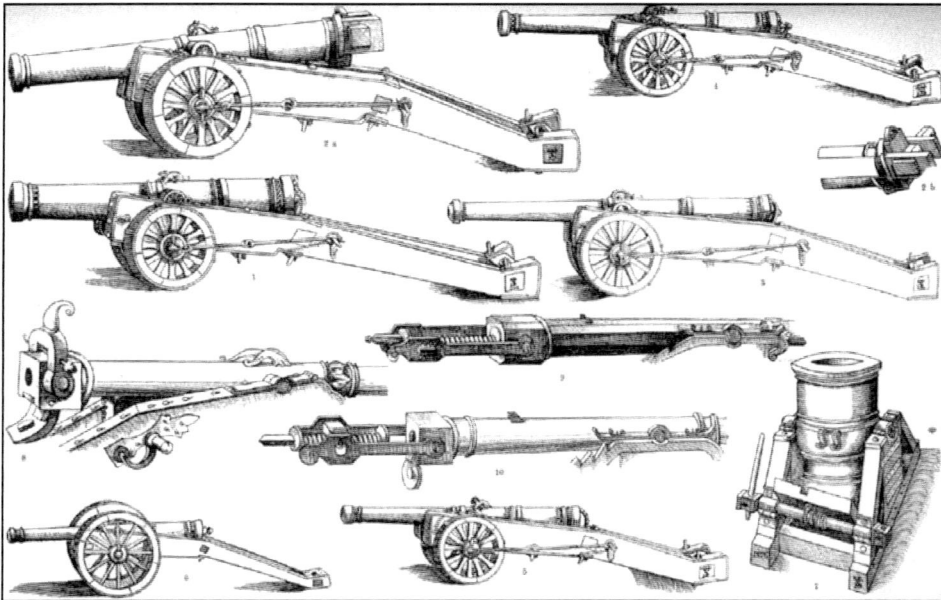

Artillery of the Period

Morale tests

Morale tests represent the results of combat. A unit can only take one morale test per turn and is only taken when acting as the passive player.

A morale test is taken by a unit when it is:

a) it is under fire (within firing range of an enemy unit)
b) it is in physical contact with an enemy unit
c) it is unsecured infantry, within ½BW of enemy cavalry, not LH.

Under Fire

To be under fire from infantry or cavalry, the friendly unit must be overlapping the front of the enemy firer; even the smallest overlap counts. Artillery can fire up to 45 degrees straight ahead and must be unlimbered to fire. Light Horse (LH) can fire from any edge or point of their base.

In all cases if any part of the enemy base is within range and angle of fire then the testing base counts as being under fire.

Ranges

 Mounted
 (D, C, H, Dr or LH, any with CS)*: ¼BW
 Foot and dismounted dragoons: ½BW
 Artillery: **3BW / 10BW** (not Light guns)

* Except for dragoons all mounted troops have the same range whether mounted or dismounted. Mounted units not listed here can fire but only in response to being fired at.

Contact with the Enemy

➤ Contact might have been initiated this turn or it may be continuing from a previous turn.
➤ Units only test morale if they are in contact with the front edge of an enemy.
➤ A unit in square can cause a test on any unit in contact but only one test. The owner chooses which unit will test.
➤ A unit in contact with an enemy cannot also test its morale for being shot at. Units providing flank support to a melee can be shot at.
➤ A unit can provide flank support to another friendly unit in melee when the two units face the same direction and are in side-edge to side-edge contact, and the supporting unit is not itself in melee.

➤ A unit proving flank support impacts the morale of the enemy unit, however, its own morale does not need testing unless another cause applies.

➤ A gun can provide fire support if within 10BW and within fire arc.

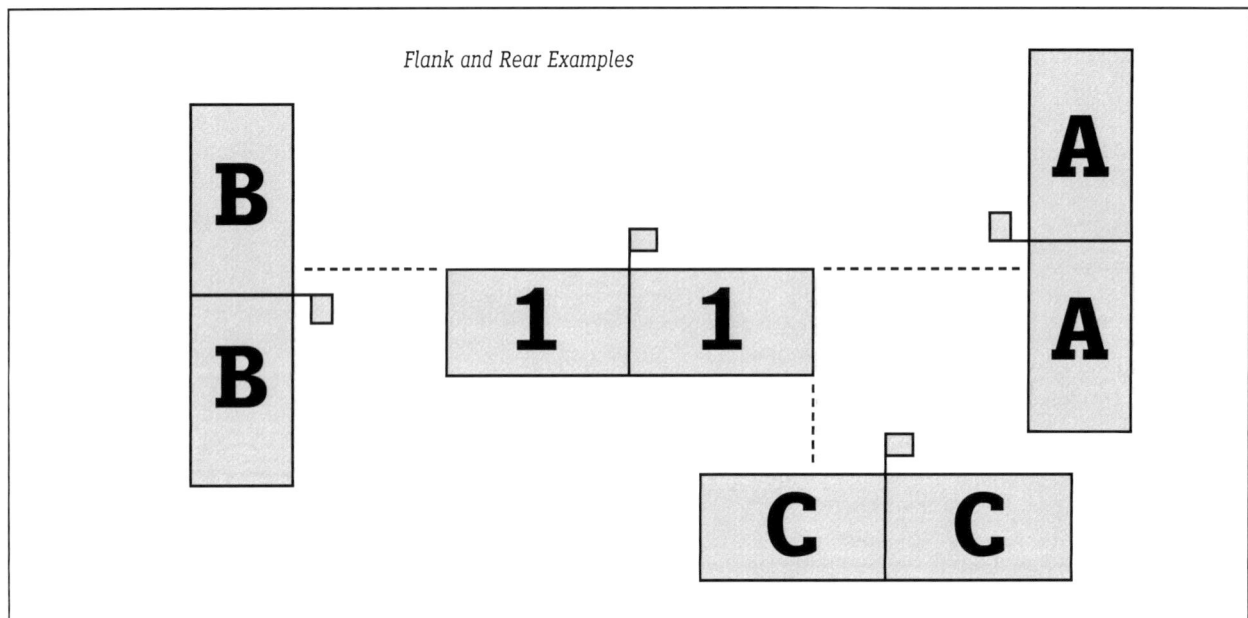

Flank and Rear Examples

Flank and Rear:

➤ **Unit A** will not count as attacking the flank of unit 1 as it does not have half its frontage behind the line across the targets front.

➤ **Unit B** would count as attacking the flank of unit 1.

➤ **Unit C** cannot count as attacking the rear of unit 1 as it does not have enough of its frontage behind the line from the flank. **Unit C** could attack the flank.

Cavalry threat:

➤ An insecure infantry unit must test if enemy cavalry (except light horse) is within ½BW.

➤ To count as secure, an infantry unit must have a friendly unit or terrain that either slows movement or gives a combat advantage within ½BW, or 1BW if the unit is a Tercio or Early Tercio, of both flanks.

➤ The friendly unit must be facing in the same general direction of the unit it is securing.

➤ The threatening cavalry must be facing generally in the direction of the unit it is threatening.

Rear Support

Armies of the period rarely risked fighting without at least one line of rear support. On table commanders should think carefully before engaging without support.

➤ A unit in line or deployed artillery has rear support if it has part of a unit in line or deployed if artillery and to its rear within ½BW if the support comes from infantry or artillery, within 1BW if from cavalry. The unit giving the support must be facing the same direction as the unit supported. Early Tercios automatically have rear support because of their size and depth.

➤ A unit in line, not deployed artillery, can have additional rear support if there are more units to the rear of units giving direct support. These units must comply with the above restrictions – i.e. be within ½BW if infantry or artillery, 1BW if cavalry, facing the same direction and partially to the rear of the first unit.

➤ These additional rear supports give a -1 modifier on the opponent's morale test. To get the second rear support bonus the front unit must have two extra units to the rear, i.e. a total of 3 units to the

rear of the front unit. This will give the opposing unit a -1 modifier in their morale test.

➤ To get the third rear support bonus the front unit must have three extra units to the rear, i.e. a total of 6 units to the rear of the front unit. This will give the opposing unit a -2 modifier overall in their morale test.

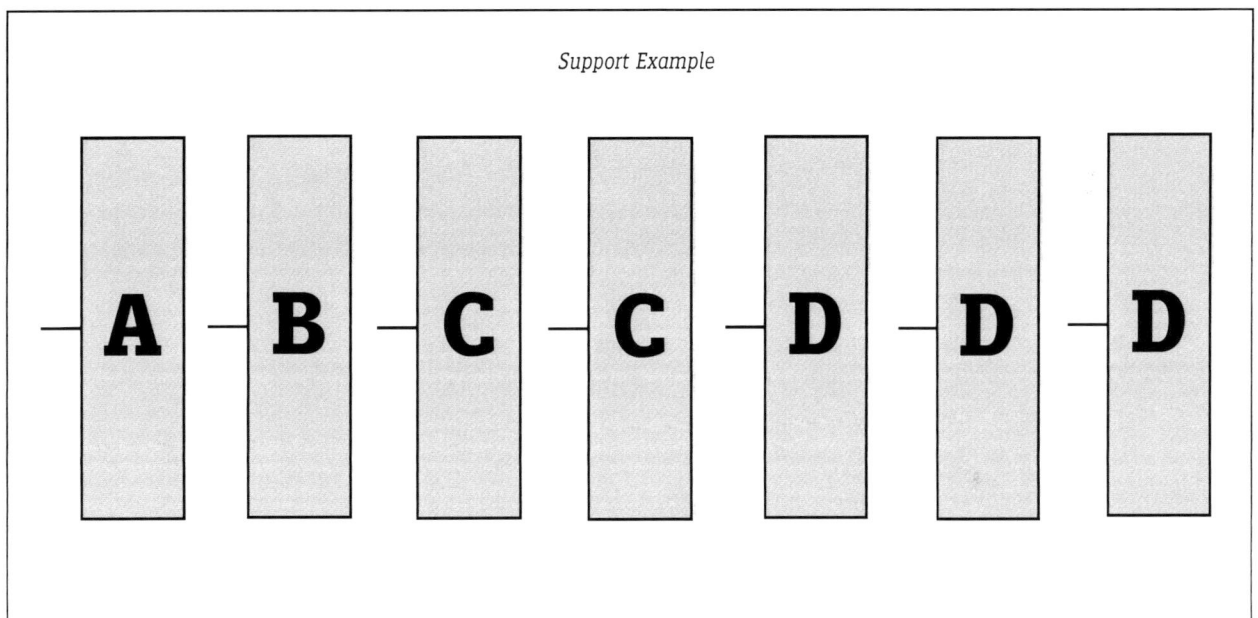

Support Example

A — B — C — C — D — D — D

Support Example:

➤ **Unit A** is in the front line. **Unit B** is close enough to give +1 rear support.

➤ You need both **C**s to be close enough behind the unit in front of them, not the front of the whole group. If they are, your unit will get the +1 rear support modifier and the opposing unit will receive a -1 modifier in their test.

➤ You then need all three **D**s as above to get the final modifier. If they are your unit will get the +1 rear support modifier and the opposing unit will receive a -2 modifier in their test.

➤ An individual column of up to 7 units (with the front unit being the one supported) one behind the next can be counted for rear support providing all the required support criteria applies.

➤ The exception to the above is Early Tercio units. These automatically get +1 rear support because of the depth of these units. They can give rear support to other units and count as 2 units above for providing support.

Morale Test Procedure

Consult the Morale Test table; add or subtract all applicable factors. Roll 2D6. Add the total dice score and the net factors to find the modified score :

▨ Modified score of 8 or more: **pass**

▨ Modified score of 4 to 7: **fail**

▨ Modified score of 3 or less: **rout**

Morale Test

Unit Quality, Size and Circumstance

+1	– Elite Unit
	– If in melee and uphill or defending terrain
	– Only fired on by artillery at more than 3BW
	– Only fired on by inferior firepower troops
	– If shot at in terrain that gives cover
-1	– Raw Unit
	– Small Unit
	– Fired on by artillery at up to ½BW
	– In column
	– For each additional reason to test above one #

Cavalry Only

-1	– Poor cavalry in contact with other cavalry
	– Cavalry the turn they are charged by Cu or Sw cavalry
	– Cavalry under fire (except LH) or in melee in bad going
	– Cavalry that pursued in contact with a fresh enemy unit
	– Dismounted cavalry or dragoons in melee with Cavalry in the open
	– Cavalry that failed to charge Du or CS in their turn and charged by said Du or CS cavalry
-2	– LH or Mounted Dragoons in melee with non LH or Mtd Dragoons
	– Cavalry the turn after being charged by Ga cavalry

Infantry Only

+1	– Infantry in Fortification
	– In square (or hedgehog) and fighting mounted
-1	– If shot at in square or hedgehog
	– Foot charged by SB that failed to charge SB in their turn**
	– Infantry, unless secure*, the turn after being charged by cavalry
	– Infantry (not PH) or artillery in melee with cavalry
	– Infantry in melee with superior melee foot
	– M infantry (unless Ma) in melee with Cavalry in the open
	– The turn after being charged by AT if the attacking unit started in musket range

Artillery Only

+1	– Artillery in Fortification
-1	– Limbered Artillery the turn after being charged by cavalry
	– Artillery in melee with cavalry

Rear Support, Flank and Rear Attack

+1	– ET providing own rear support
	– Rear Support (within ½BW for Inf./Art., 1BW for Cavalry)
-1	– For each additional reason to test above one, including flank and fire support and additional enemy rear support after the first
	– At least one enemy element entirely behind flank within 2BW (unless the unit is enemy LH)
-2	– At least one enemy element entirely behind flank within 2BW (unless the unit is enemy LH) (ET only -1)
	– If enemy unit is in contact with flank OR rear, (ET only get -1 if in flank)

* Secured infantry: Infantry that has another friendly unit or terrain that slows movement or gives a combat advantage within ½BW (1BW if T or ET) of both flanks.
** To clarify this, the sequence would be : a mounted unit attempts to charge into combat with a D unit or a unit with attached CS but fails the Action Test or tests to contact. On the next friendly turn, the D unit (or a unit with attached CS) successfully charges. On the following turn, the unit that initially failed to charge gets the -1. The same is true with foot units and SB units.
# This applies to for every additional unit that is firing, bombarding, in physical contact with or for each additional cavalry unit within ½BW or unsecure infantry. An individual unit can only count in a single morale test, whether as the cause of the test or as flank support. If the unit has a choice it must cause a test.

Inferior Firepower

If a unit is being fired on by a unit that has inferior firepower, then it receives a +1 modifier. The ranking, from best to worst, is:

1. M
2. MH and dismounted dragoons
3. MX and Harquebusier Cavalry
4. PH
5. Other mounted firers – Dutch, Cuirassier, all other mounted with CS
6. Light Horse, mounted dragoons
7. All others

If a unit has regimental guns, its ranking improves by one level. *Example: a MX unit with regimental guns counts as rank 2.*

If cavalry that can fire has commanded shot, its ranking improves by one level. **Example:** *Dutch cavalry with Commanded Shot count as rank 4.*

Arquebus-armed units drop one level. *Example: MH infantry armed with Arquebus count as rank 3.*

Superior Melee Foot

If a foot unit is in melee with a foot unit that has a Superior Melee rating, then the unit receives this -1 modifier. The ranking, from best to worst, is:

1. PH
2. MX
3. MH
4. M

If the unit is AT foot, then its ranking improves by one level. *Example: a MH unit with AT counts as rank 2.*

Morale Test Examples

A 'Regiment' infantry unit has an enemy cavalry unit to its front within ½BW. They count as a threat and it must take a morale test. The unit is trained and it has rear support. The infantry get +1 for the support and roll a 7, so the final score is 8 and they pass the test.

A cavalry unit is within ½BW of an enemy Tercio infantry unit so it is under fire and must test. The unit is trained and has rear support but there is also an artillery unit firing from 8BW away. The unit has +1 for rear support but -1 for the artillery and -1 for cavalry under fire, so -1 overall. The player rolls 8 -1 = 7, the test is failed and the unit loses one of its allowed morale fails.

A trained MH infantry unit has an enemy cavalry unit in contact with it, it moved into contact the previous enemy phase. The infantry unit does not have a secure flank or rear support. The attacking cavalry has a supporting unit and this is entirely behind the units flank. The unit gets -1 for being charged and not having secure flanks, -1 for in melee with cavalry, -1 for the additional enemy unit and a further -1 for the unit to its flank – a total of -4. It rolls 7 -4 = 3. The unit routs and is removed from play.

Morale Test Outcomes

Pass
The unit carries on as normal, with no ill effects.

Fail
A unit can suffer only so many morale fails before it is broken and is removed from play. Each fail is marked on the unit. It is removed when it reaches:

Morale Failures Before Routing

Troop type	Cu	Hq	Sw	Du	Ga	LH	Dr	ET	Tc	SB	Rt
No. failures	3	3	2	2	2	2	2	5	4	4	3

The above is modified by the following:

- Large units suffer an extra fail before routing.
- Determined units suffer an extra fail before routing.
- Wavering units suffer one less fail before routing.
- Artillery routs on a 2nd fail or if it fails whilst in contact with an enemy base.

Example: *a Wavering Regiment unit routs on its 2nd morale failure.*

Example: *a Determined or Large Regiment unit would only break on its 4th failure.*

Rout
A unit is removed from play immediately if it gets a rout result.

Generals and morale tests
A general attached to a unit may re-roll one morale test per turn but the new result must be applied even if worse than the first result. If a General is within 1BW, then he may to attach to a unit. If a unit is forced to re-align, then a General may attach to it if he was within 1BW prior to the re-alignment.

A General attached to a unit is killed if an unmodified 4 is rolled on the morale test of that unit. A General that is killed is replaced the following turn by another General with a (0) rating.

Unattached Generals that are contacted by enemy units are moved out of contact towards the nearest friendly unit.

Breaking Off Contact

Infantry Break Off
If infantry is contacted by other infantry it can withdraw ¼BW after a successful morale test. If the unit is occupying defences or terrain it can force the opposing unit to pull back this distance instead.

Artillery Break Off
If an artillery unit is contacted it can choose to shelter with a friendly unit. The gun model remains in place but the crew join a friendly unit within 1BW and shelter within it, this is a free action and is immediate. The exact unit must be indicated and if that unit is lost then the artillery unit is lost too. The crew may return to the gun model on any subsequent turn but this is an action.

Cavalry Break Off

If a Cavalry unit in contact with an enemy fails its Morale test, then it must break contact. Break off is compulsory. No Action test is required, even in circumstances where it normally would be. The maximum break off move is 6BW, but how far a unit actually travels depends on whether it has rear support or not:

- If the failing unit has rear support within 6BW, then it is placed behind that unit, facing the enemy.
- If the unit has no rear support within 6BW, then it about faces and moves straight backwards 6BW and remains facing away from the enemy.

All cavalry units that break off cannot move in their next turn (the break off move is, in effect, their next turn, even though it is performed immediately).

A unit that is breaking off will retreat through a gap if one is available (see zones of control page 23); however, if its path is entirely blocked by enemy units and ZOCs, then the retreating unit is removed from play and considered destroyed.

Light Horse Pull Back

To reflect their greater mobility, Light Horse units have the chance to pull back from contact if charged or if already in a melee.

If a friendly Light Horse unit is already in contact with an enemy, then it can pull back to a position ¼BW from the final position of the enemy unit. It remains facing the enemy unit. No Action Test is required; the player simply moves the unit.

If an enemy unit comes into contact with a friendly Light Horse unit, then the Light Horse can attempt to pull back to avoid contact. It immediately takes an Action Test. If it passes, it moves away ¼BW from where the charging unit halted. If it fails, then it will have to take a morale test; if it is still in

contact during its next movement phase it can automatically pull back.

Pursuit

Only cavalry units are permitted to pursue; units on foot do not pursue. Dragoons also never pursue (this reflects their status as mounted infantry, rather than being true cavalry). Some scenarios may vary the normal conditions e.g. Highlanders may pursue.

A cavalry unit that can pursue, will pursue—unless it passes a pursuit test to stop it pursuing.

There are two situations in which a friendly cavalry unit might pursue :

- When an enemy unit fails its morale test whilst in contact with a friendly cavalry unit
- When an enemy Wing fails a morale test

Pursuing a Unit

A friendly cavalry unit in contact with an enemy unit that has fallen back or routed will pursue unless it takes and passes a pursuit test. If it does not pursue, then there are no further consequences. If it does pursue, then friendly units that provided it with flank or rear support might also pursue, depending on whether there is Pursuit Contact or a Breakthrough (see below).

Pursuing a Wing

If an enemy Wing fails its Wing Morale test, then this might also trigger pursuit. Which friendly units are affected is determined at the moment the Wing fails. Any friendly unit eligible to pursue that is closer to any unit in the Wing that has failed the test than to other enemy units must test. The measurement is taken from the nearest point of the friendly unit to the nearest point of the enemy units.

Pursuit Test

Pursuit tests are taken immediately after the opposing unit breaks off or routs, or at the moment an enemy Wing fails its Morale test.

Each unit testing to not pursue rolls a D6 and adds or subtracts these modifiers:

+1 testing unit is Trained
+2 testing unit is Raw
+2 testing unit is Gallopers
-1 General within 1BW
-2 testing unit is Wavering.

Outcome: modified score is 3 or less: no pursuit; remain in position
modified score is 4 or more: pursue.

Pursuit Distance

The maximum distance a unit pursues is determined by a modified dice roll. Roll a D6 and add the following modifiers:

+1 unit is Trained
+2 unit is Raw
+4 unit is Galloper

The result is the maximum number ofBW the unit will move in its pursuit.

The pursuing unit moves directly forward until one of the following occurs:

- It has used up its pursuit distance and there are still enemy units ahead of it.
- It contacts an enemy unit (see Pursuit Contact).
- Until it has no enemy units directly in front of it and it has passed through the enemy line (see Breakthrough).

Pursuit Contact

The pursuing unit must contact any enemy unit even partially in its path. It does not need an Action Test to do this. As the pursuers are disordered, this contact is not considered to be a charge for future morale test purposes and the pursuing unit also receives a -1 modifier in its subsequent morale test.

If the pursuing unit does contact an enemy unit, then the pursuit halts. Also, any flank or rear supporting units do not have to test to pursue.

Breakthrough

When the pursuing unit passes through the enemy line, then a Breakthrough has occurred. On breaking through, the friendly unit continues its pursuit by diverting up to 45 degrees in the direction of the baggage, or the centre of the enemy rear table edge if there is no baggage marker.

If a friendly unit breaks through, then any eligible friendly units that were providing it with flank or rear support must also pursue or test to avoid pursuit.

Light Horse and Pursuit

If it is in contact with an enemy that fails its morale test or routs, Light Horse may choose whether to pursue or not; it does not have to test for pursuit. Similarly, if an enemy Wing fails its morale test, Light Horse may choose to pursue or not. However, if there is a Breakthrough, then Light Horse tests for pursuit just like other cavalry. This reflects the desire of Light Horse to get at the enemy baggage.

Pursuit Examples

Example 1: The mounted unit contacted by an Elite Galloper unit with flank and rear support fails its morale test and breaks off behind its own rear support. The Elite Gallopers roll a D6 to avoid pursuit. It rolls a 3 and adds 2 because it is Gallopers = 5, the unit pursues. It rolls a D6, scores 1, and adds 4 (because it is Gallopers) so its maximum pursuit distance is 5BW. In the event, it only moves 2BW before contacting the former rear support of the opposing unit. Because the unit has contacted another opposing unit the friendly units providing flank and rear support do not need to test for pursuit.

Example 2: Later in the game, the same unit still with flank and rear support routs an opposing unit. It pursues, but this time there is no immediate support for the opposing unit (there are opposing units to one flank but nothing in front of them in the pursuit path). The pursuing unit rolls for its pursuit distance: it rolls 3 and adds 4 because it is Gallopers = 7BW. The unit moves 2BW forward to a position behind the line of the opposing units to the flank. It now turns up to 45 degrees in the direction of the baggage and moves the remaining 5BW in that direction. Because the unit in contact has made a Breakthrough, both the flank and rear supporting units test to avoid pursuit. The unit to the rear passes but the one to the flank fails. This unit is a Trained Swedish cavalry. It rolls for how far it will pursue and adds 1 because it is trained. It rolls 3 plus 1 for trained = 4BW. It moves forward 2BW to clear the enemy lines. Then it turns up to 45 degrees towards the baggage and moves a further 2BW.

Wing morale test

When a wing has lost half (or more) of its units, then it has to test its morale. This is not a one-off : it must test every turn from now on. Roll 1D6 and add the Wing Commander's rating:

▨ Total is 4 or more: **Pass; wing carries on.**
▨ Total is 3 or less: **Fail; all wing units are removed from play.**

Army morale test

When an army has lost half (or more) of its Wings, then it has to test its morale. From this move on, it rolls each turn it loses another wing. Roll 1D6 and add the Army Commander's rating:

▨ Total is 5 or more: **Pass; army carries on.**
▨ Total is 4 or less: **Fail; army is defeated; remove all units.**

The Battle of Naseby, 1645

Twilight of Divine Right

Build Your Own Armies

This is a system for generating typical armies for players who wish to make up their own scenario. The lists are based, roughly, on the forces available to the two main ECW armies, the Oxford Royalists and Essex's army (New Model Army from 1645). The players choose a year and then roll for how many units of each type they have in their army.

The tables give enough units for around 4 hours play on a 1.8m by 1.2m table, 6 foot by 4 foot, if using aBW of 60mm.

If less time or space is available, roll for the number of units but halve the total and round up. To illustrate the process after each section there will be an example of what to do using the 1643 Royalist army.

Parliamentarian Infantry

	1642	1643	1644	1645
No. of Units	8 + D6	5 + D6	5 + D6	5 + D6
Weapon Ratio (D6)	1-2 MX, 3-6 MH	1 MX, 2-5 MH, 6 M	1-5 MH, 6 M	
Unit Size (D6 +1 if M)	1 Large, 6 Small			
Quality (D6 +1 if M)	Raw	1-2 R, 3-5 T, 6 E	1 R, 2-5 T, 6 E	1-4 R, 5-6 T

Royalist Infantry

	1642	1643	1644	1645
No. of Units	6 + D6	4 + D6	4 + (D6/2)	4 + (D6 − 1)
Weapon Ratio	1-5: PH	1-2: MX	1: MX 2-5: MH 6: M	
(roll 1D6 per unit)	6: MX	3-5: MH, 6: M		
Unit Size (D6 +1 if M)	6: Small	5+: Small	4+: Small	2+: Small
Quality (D6 +1 if M)	Raw	1: R , 2-5: T, 6: E	1: R, 2-4: T, 5-6 : E	1-3: T 4-6: E

In 1645 all the Royalists are AT

Example: The player is creating a 1643 Royalist army and rolls a D6 for the number of infantry units in the army and adds 4. The player rolls 3 and so has 7 infantry units. If a smaller game is planned this number would be halved and rounded up to 4. The players intend using a full army and so now the Royalist player rolls for the details of each unit. For each unit the player rolls 3 times to establish the weapon ratio, unit size and quality.

For the first unit the player rolls a 5, a 4 and a 1 so the unit is MH standard sized and Raw. For the 2nd unit his first roll is a 6, a M unit. Because it is a M unit it receives a +1 modifier to the next roll and gets a 4, modified to 5 and so the unit is Small. It also receives a +1 modifier on the Quality roll. The player rolls a 1, modified to a 2. The unit is therefore Trained, Small and M. The player now rolls for the other units.

Parliamentarian Cavalry

	1642	1643	1644	1645
No. of Units	1 + D6	7 + D6	8 + D6	7 + D6
Type (D6)	1-5 Dutch, 6 Swedish		1-4 Du., 5-6 Swed.	1 Dutch, 2-6 Swed.
Unit Size	6 Small		1 Large, 6 Small	
Quality (D6)	1-5 R, 6 T	1-2 R, 3- 6 T	1 R, 2-5 T, 6 E	1 R, 2-4 T, 5- 6 E

Royalist Cavalry

	1642	1643	1644	1645
No. of Units	1 + D6	9 + D6	5 + D6	8 + D6
Type	Galloper	Swedish		
Unit Size	6 Small		5-6 Small	2-6 Small
Quality (D6)	1-5 R, 6 T	1-2 R, 3-5 T, 6 E	1 R, 2-4 T, 5-6 E	1-3 T, 4-6 E

Cavalry can have Commanded Shot (CS) by adjusting the ratings of infantry in the army. If a unit is Small it is downgraded one level of shot – M become MH, MH become MX, etc. – and 1 cavalry unit can have CS. If a unit is not Small it can be downgraded one level of shot as above and also downgrade one size level – Large become standard, standard becomes Small. Each downgrade provides 1 cavalry unit with a CS.

Example: Having determined the infantry in the army the player now rolls for the cavalry. He rolls a D6 and scores a 1, therefore there are 10 cavalry in the army. The player does not need to roll for type as they are all Swedish-style cavalry. They will need to roll twice each for the unit size and quality. The player rolls for his 1st cavalry unit and scores a 2 and a 6: the unit is a standard-sized Elite Swedish Cavalry. The player now rolls for the other units. The Royalist player decides

Mounted Sword Drill

he needs some CS to support the cavalry. It is decided to downgrade two of the infantry units he rolled above. The Trained, Small, M unit is downgraded to MH and provide a CS to 1 cavalry unit. The Raw Standard MH can be downgraded twice to Raw Small MX and this will provide 2 CS for cavalry units.

Parliamentarian Dragoons

	1642	1643	1644	1645
No. of Units (D6)	2-3: 1 unit, 4+ 2 units	5+ 1 unit	5+ 1 unit	2+ 1 unit
Unit Size (D6)	1 Standard, 2+ Small			1 or 2 Standard, 3+ Large
Quality (D6)	Raw	1 Raw, 2+Trained		Trained

Royalist Dragoons

	1642	1643	1644	1645
No. of Units (D6)	2-3: 1 unit, 4+ 2 units	5+ 1 unit	3+ 1 unit	5+ 1 unit
Unit Size (D6)	1 Standard, 2+ Small			
Quality (D6)	Raw	1 Raw, 2+Trained		Trained

Example: The Royalist player now rolls to see if any dragoon units are with the army. He rolls a 4 so there isn't (a roll of 5 or more and there would have been).

Artillery

	1642	1643	1644	1645
No. of Units (D6)	1-3: 2 units, 4 or 5: 1 unit, 6: none			
Quality	Trained			

The player may choose not to use 1 or more guns and have Regimental Guns (RGs) instead. Removing 1 gun allows up to 4 infantry units to have RGs.

Example: The Royalist player now rolls for the number of field guns with the army. He rolls 3 so he has 2 field guns. All field guns are Trained. The player decides to remove 1 of the guns and so 4 of his infantry units will now have RGs.

Commanders

If the player has an army of up to 10 units use 1 commander, the army commander. For each additional 5 units, use one additional commander, up to a maximum of three.

Example: an army with 13 units has an army commander and 1 other commander.

Example: an army with 21 units has an army commander and 3 other commanders.

Each commander should control at least ¼ of the available units. If the army has 2 additional commanders, then the army commander does not have to directly command any troops, or he can command less than ¼ of those available (probably the Reserve).

- If the army has 2 commanders the army will fight as 2 Wings, 1 under the direct command of the army commander.
- If the army has 3 commanders it can fight as 3 Wings, 1 under the direct command of the army commander. Alternatively the bulk of the army can be in 2 Wings under additional commanders while the army commanders either doesn't directly control anything or only a small Reserve.
- It the army has 4 commanders it will fight as 4 Wings with the army commander not directly controlling anything or only a small Reserve.

Roll a D6 for the ability of each commander and use the following tables.

Parliamentarian Commander Ratings

	1642	1643	1644	1645
Army Commander	1-5: 1, 6: 0		1: 2, 2-5: 1, 6: 0	1-5: 2, 6: 1
Wing Commander	1: 2, 2-5: 1, 6: 0		1-2: 2, 3-5: 1, 6: 0	

Royalist Commander Ratings

	1642	1643	1644	1645
Army Commander	1: 2, 2-5: 1, 6: 0			1: 3, 2-5: 2, 6: 1
Wing Commander	1-3: 2, 4-5: 1, 6: 0		1-2: 2, 3-5: 1, 6: 0	1-2: 2, 3-5: 1, 6: 0

Example: The Royalist player has 7 infantry units, 10 cavalry units and 1 field gun, a total of 18 units so the player will have an Army Commander and 2 additional commanders. Each commander is now rolled for to determine his ability. The Army Commander rolls a 3 and so has an ability of 1 (probably King Charles). For the additional commanders, the player rolls a 2 and a 5: one commander has a rating of 2 (perhaps Prince Rupert) and another of 1 (one of a number of other available commanders).

The player decides to use three commands representing the centre, right and left Wings. Each wing should have at least ¼ of the available units, in this case 5 units. The 1 ability additional commander is assigned 5 of the cavalry units, including those with CS attached. These will be the Left Wing of the army. The remaining cavalry, 5 units, are assigned to the 2 ability additional commander along with 1 of the infantry unit to provide some fire support. These will be the Right Wing. The other 6 infantry units and the field gun will be the Centre under the Army Commander.

Introductory Scenario 1

The Battle of Fleurus, 29th August 1622

In 1622 the Protestant cause was in disarray after a string of defeats in the early stages of the Thirty Years War. Earlier in 1622, three Protestant armies had attempted to recapture the lost lands of Frederick of the Palatinate, a leading Protestant, but without success. The remnants of two of the armies involved in this under Mansfeld and Christian of Brunswick withdrew and regrouped, intending to move north to the Netherlands through Spanish Flanders. On August 27th the vanguard of the Protestant army ran into Spanish outposts. After some skirmishes, and with growing discontent within the ranks, it was clear that the Protestants would need to fight. The Spanish army had taken up a position near to Fleurus and Mansfeld moved to attack them.

Mansfeld led an army with a considerable numerical advantage over Cordoba's Spanish. His army was 10,000 to 11,000 strong, about 5,000 cavalry and 5,000 to 6,000 infantry. He also had 11 guns but most of these were not at the battle. Cordoba only had 8,000 to 8,500 men, 6,000 infantry and 2,000 to 2,500 cavalry, and 4 or 7 guns. Yet numbers were not everything. Mansfeld's army was largely using the new tactics developed by Maurice of Nassau but the troops were relatively inexperienced and discontent was rife. In contrast, Cordoba's army contained many veterans. It was true they were using older tactics but the infantry in particular had a fearsome reputation. They were to prove their worth again in this battle.

Map

The map is 20BW by 20BW. With aBW of 60mm this would be 1.2m by 1.2m (4' by 4').

Terrain

The **high ground** gives the uphill bonus in melee. The **woods** are bad going. The **chateau and grounds** around it count as defensive terrain and uphill in melee. They are also cover if fired upon. They are large enough for a single unit.

The baggage requires an Action Test to enter and another to exit. It does not provide any defensive bonuses.

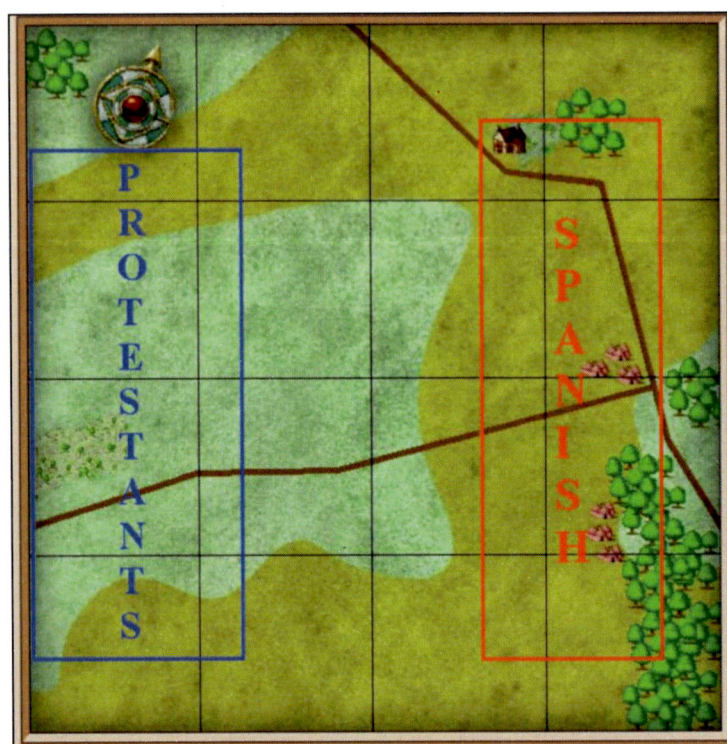

Scenario

The Protestant army was discontented and about half of the Right Wing cavalry refused to fight. The Protestant player has a choice:

- He could just assign half of the units of the Right Wing as mutineers; that is one unit of Cuirassiers and two units of Dutch style cavalry, one Trained (C) and one Trained (D), or
- He can roll a D6 per unit and on a 1, 2 or 3 result that unit is in Mutiny. This could of course lead to more or less than half of them revolting.

Included in the Protestant army is some artillery. This was not involved in the battle but can be used for 'what if' or similar scenarios.

Orders of Battle

The Spanish Army: Cordoba (2)

Left Wing (cavalry in 2 lines):
1 Trained (A), Small, M Regiment (in the Chateau)
1 Trained (D), Cuirassier
1 Trained (D), Small, Harquebusier

Centre:
1 Elite, MX Tercio
2 Trained (B), Small, MX Tercio
1 Trained (A), MX Tercio
1 Trained Field Gun

Right Wing (cavalry in 2 lines):
1 Trained (B), Cuirassier
1 Trained (C), Small, Harquebusier

Baggage is on the centre of the rear table edge behind the army.

The Protestant Army: Mansfeld (1)

Right Wing (2 Lines):
2 Trained (C), Cuirassiers
2 Trained (C), Dutch Cavalry
2 Trained (D), Dutch Cavalry

Centre:
1 Trained (C), Large, MX Regiment
2 Trained (C), MX Regiment
2 Trained (D), MX Regiment
1 Trained Field Gun

Left Wing (2 Lines):
1 Trained (C), Small, Cuirassiers
2 Trained (C), Dutch Cavalry
1 Trained (D), Dutch Cavalry

Baggage is on the centre of the rear table edge behind the army.

Victory Conditions

The Spanish win if they are undefeated by the end of the battle.

Introductory Scenario 2

The Battle of Cheriton, 29th March 1644

In early 1644 a Royalist army under Hopton and a Parliamentarian army under Waller were campaigning in southern England. After some manoeuvring, both sides received reinforcements. The Royalists were joined by a contingent from the Oxford Army under the Earl of Forth while Waller received assistance from some units of London Trained Band foot and cavalry from Essex's army under Balfour. Both sides continued indecisive manoeuvres until they confronted each other at Cheriton in Hampshire.

The exact reason for and location of the battle is debatable but in this scenario I have followed the view of Malcolm Wanklyn ('Decisive Battles of the English Civil War', 2006). Whatever was the case, what followed was a sharply fought small battle and is a useful initial scenario.

Map

The map is 20BW by 20BW. With aBW of 60mm this would be 1.2 m by 1.2m (4' by 4')

Terrain

The **high ground** gives the uphill bonus in melee. The South Spur is the highest ground and blocks line of sight from other heights. The North Spur and Hinton Ampner Ridge are higher than the Middle Spur.

The woods and villages count as defensive terrain and cover for a unit on foot.

The **area of enclosures and heath** counts as bad going but can be entered by mounted troops as well as foot. Mounted troops move as foot in bad going. The enclosures and heath count as defensive terrain for a unit on foot.

The **stream** is an Action Test to cross and is defensive terrain in melee.

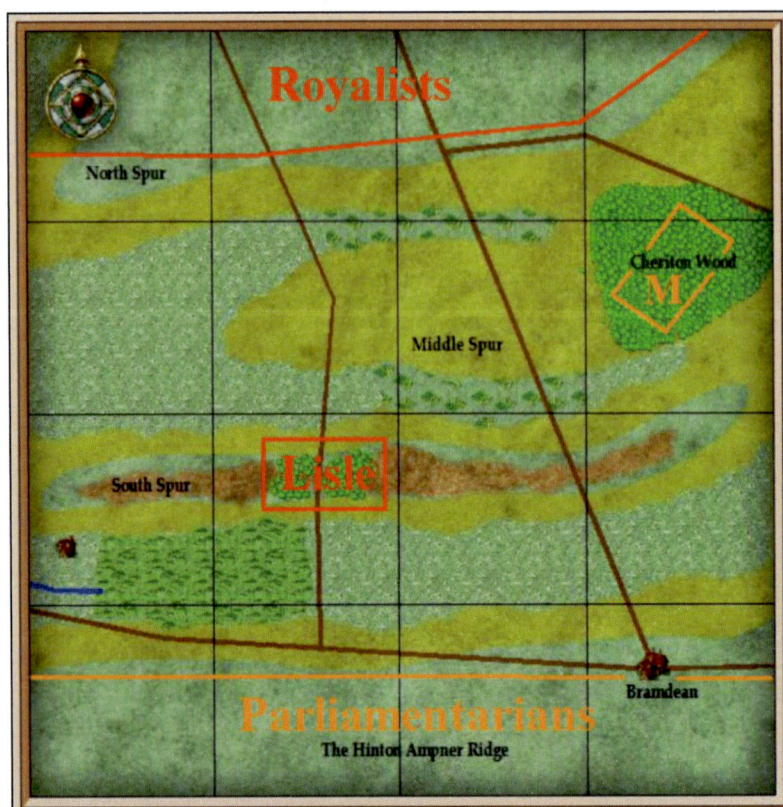

Scenario

All infantry are 'Regiment' type. The Parliamentarians move first.

Deployment: The armies are deployed in the areas marked 'Royalists' and 'Parliamentarians' but each side has a unit detached elsewhere. In 'M' the Parliamentarians have their Trained (C), M unit of detached musketeers. In 'Lisle' the Royalist must deploy a single MX or MH infantry unit.

Bard's Advance: Bard's regiment made an unordered advance which may have precipitated the battle. After the two sides have deployed but before the game starts, the Parliamentarian player can move one of the Royalist Trained (C), Small units. This unit will move 1D6BW straight forward, ignoring terrain. However, it stops if it would come within 3 ½BW of any enemy troops. The battle then commences.

Orders of Battle

The Royalist Army

Joint Army Commanders*:
Hopton (1)
Forth (1)

Left Wing Hopton's troops:

Infantry:	1 Elite, Small, AT, M (Detached Musketeers)
	2 Trained (C), Small, MX
Artillery:	1 Trained Field Gun
Cavalry:	2 Trained (B), Large, Swedish Cavalry
	2 Trained (B), Swedish Cavalry

Right Wing Forth's troops:

Infantry:	1 Trained (C), Small, MH
Cavalry:	2 Trained (B), Swedish Cavalry

Baggage is on the centre of the rear table edge behind the army.

* It is not clear whether Hopton or Forth (if either) was in overall command so the player can choose either of these as the army commander. The player must assign the troops to a specific commander before the game. Each commander has 1 of the guns under his command and at least 4 other units. Up to four units can be swapped between commands at the start if the battle.

The Parliamentarian Army

Army Commander:
Waller (1)

Infantry under Waller:
1 Trained (C), M (Detached Musketeers - M)
3 Trained (D), MX (Waller's Foot)
1 Trained (C), MX (London Trained Band)
1 Trained Field Gun

Cavalry Balfour (1):
2 Trained (B), Dutch Cavalry
4 Trained (C), Dutch Cavalry
1 Trained (D), Dragoon

Baggage is on the centre of the rear table edge behind the army.

Victory Conditions

The Royalists win if they are undefeated by the end of the battle.

Optional Rules

The Brigade Scale

This scale is appropriate for the larger battles of the period; Breitenfeld is a prime example. In game terms, the only thing that changes is the ratio of real to tabletop units; all the rules and distances remain the same. 1BW is approximately 300 metres.

A unit represents a brigade or its equivalent which equates to approximately 2,000 to 4,000 infantry or 1,000 to 1,600 cavalry. 1 artillery unit is used for each 20 guns or part thereof in the army, so an army with 22 guns would field 2 artillery units. 1 siege artillery unit is used for each 10 guns or part thereof in the army.

Variable Unit Sizes

The inclusion of variable unit sizes allows the scenario designer the flexibility to tailor the scenario to suit historical circumstances.

If it had fewer units, an historical army could spread its units out to avoid being outflanked. On other occasions, the individual battalia or squadrons could be significantly smaller or larger than was generally the case. Another example of this would be a unit of mounted troops who have dismounted. The effective combat strength of the unit would now be less than normal. Finally, the unit depicted might be a different size for some tactical reason: it might be a small detachment occupying a vital position or, on the other hand, it might have been reinforced to assault a position.

Scenario designers should limit variation to not greater than 20% larger or smaller than the standard size as this has an impact on the system and scale. If an historical unit is larger than this, it would be better to field it as two game units instead. Similarly, if a unit is too small, it is better to combine it with one of more other units to create a single game unit.

Variable Quality

The standard system is: units that are clearly inferior or superior to the norm are rated as Raw or Elite, with the great majority being 'Trained.' The Variable Quality roll means that some will perform better and some will perform worse than that on the day. This is noted by giving these units an additional rating – so a unit might be Trained (B) or Trained (D), for example. Units which ought to be better than average will be Trained (B) and are more likely to be rated as Elite. Players will see from the table below that a Trained (B) unit has a ⅓rd chance of actually being Elite and a 1/6th chance of being Raw.

The quality of the unit is determined by rolling 1D6. This could be done before deployment or after deployment but before the game stars. The recommended method, however, is to not roll for Variable Quality until the unit first has to take a morale test. Once the quality is decided it remains the same during the battle.

Random Quality Table

Rating	1	2	3	4	5	6
Trained (A)	Trained	Trained	Trained	Trained	Elite	Elite
Trained (B)	Raw	Trained	Trained	Trained	Elite	Elite
Trained (C)	Raw	Trained	Trained	Trained	Trained	Elite
Trained (D)	Raw	Raw	Trained	Trained	Trained	Elite
Trained (E)	Raw	Raw	Trained	Trained	Trained	Trained

Average Dice

In an earlier version of these rules, morale tests and pursuit distances used Average dice (numbered 2 3 3 4 4 5). The rules now use D6s only but, if they choose, players can use Average dice instead. Still roll one or two dice as specified in individual rule section, but now use these (slightly) amended outcomes of the morale test instead:

Add the total dice score and the net factors to find the modified score :

- Modified score of 8 or more: **Pass.**
- Modified score of 5 to 7: **Fail.**
- Modified score of 4 or less: **Rout.**

The Pike and Shot Society

Founded in 1973, the Pike and Shot Society is an international organisation that promotes interest in the warfare of the Early Modern Period, a time that saw radical change in the way in which wars were fought worldwide. It publishes a highly respected bi-monthly journal, *Arquebusier*, and a number of specialist books, monographs and booklets.

Pike & Shot Warfare

The Society takes its name from the predominant weapons of the period, from the first massed use of handguns (shot) by the Hussites of Bohemia in the early fifteenth century, to the end of the Great Northern War in 1721, which saw the demise of the pike as a frontline battlefield weapon.

This period was, like others a time of transition, to the extent that historians refer to it as the Military Revolution, whether they subscribe to that thesis or not. Despite this academic recognition, we believe that the period does not receive the popular recognition it deserves. The Society seeks to correct that shortfall.

The most well known conflict of the era in this country is the English Civil War(s), often labelled the British Civil Wars. On the continent of Europe, particularly in German culture, the Thirty Years' War is dominant and has resonance today. These may be the Early Modern Period's most recognised wars, but the Society seeks to promote interest across the whole period. The Conquistadors and the Amerindians (such as Aztecs and Incas) provide a change of geography. Back in Europe, at the same time, the Swiss pike block reached its zenith, before being successfully countered by the combined arms of the Spanish Tercio. Despite its dominance, the Spanish military juggernaut could not crush the breakaway Dutch Provinces in eighty years of siege warfare. In the Far East, Japanese Samurai warfare attained its most sophisticated flowering. The French Wars of Religion witnessed the resurgence of the mounted arm, now with pistols rather than edged weapons.

The latter part of the Society's area of interest sees the rise of military professionalism in the army of Louis XIV and the construction of coalitions by other states to fight France to a standstill, culminating in the War of the Spanish Succession. The concurrent Great Northern War saw similar mass involvement by the powers of Northern and Eastern Europe. Finally, as if that were not enough, there is the naval aspect of the period, including Lepanto, the Spanish Armada and the titanic clashes of the seventeenth century that defined the three Anglo-Dutch Wars.

Membership of the Pike & Shot Society

Members receive the Society's journal, *Arquebusier*, once every two months. A typical issue has 48 pages and includes several articles, colour illustrations and reviews of products in the Society's period of interest. It reflects the interests and research of the Society's members, and other military historians too. Authors offer material free of charge so the Society is able to keep its subscription to the minimum.

In addition to *Arquebusier*, Pike and Shot Society members benefit from discounts on a wide range of books and other products of interest. These range from reprints of contemporary documents to booklets on particular aspects of the period to very handsome volumes on uniforms and flags.

Although based in Great Britain, it remains an important aim of the Society to recruit members from around the world. The international nature of the Society means that it has access to a very wide range of material, which it publishes for the benefit of members.

Further details can be found on the Society's website: www.pikeandshot.org